BILLY GRAHAM

A note from Billy Graham

For many years I have sought to walk with God every day. What a joy it is to wake up in the morning and know He is with me, no matter what the day has in store. What a joy it is to look back in the evening and be able to thank Him for His faithfulness and to experience His peace. What a joy it is to know that some day soon the burdens of this life will be over and I will awaken in His presence!

When I think about God's love I tend to dwell upon all the good things He has done for me. But then I must stop and realize that even when circumstances have been hard or the way unclear, God has still surrounded me with His love. God's love is just as real and just as powerful in the darkness as it is in the light. And that is why we can have hope!

Every day I turn to the Bible to give me strength and wisdom for the day and hope for the future. Its words have seen me through good times and bad—through times of happiness and grief, health and sickness, victory and disappointment. God's Word can do the same for you. May God use these selections to encourage you and give you hope. May they also challenge you both to live more fully for Christ and to trust His great love—no matter what comes your way.

— BILLY GRAHAM

Joyful, joyful, we adore Thee,
God of glory, Lord of love;
Hearts unfold like flowers before Thee,
Opening to the sun above.

Joyous Optimism

My soul shall be joyful in the LORD.

PSALM 35:9

When Jesus Christ is the source of our joy, no words can describe it. It is a joy "inexpressible and glorious" (1 Pet. 1:8, NIV). Christ is the answer to the sadness and discouragement, the discord and division in our world. He can take discouragement and despondence out of our lives and replace them with optimism and hope.

If our hearts have been attuned to God through an abiding faith in Christ, the result will be joyous optimism and good cheer. The reason? Because we know He loves us, and nothing "shall be able to separate us from the love of God which is in Christ Jesus our Lord" (Rom. 8:39).

When our confidence is in Him, discouragement gets crowded out. May that be true in your life today!

A Treasury of Faith

Why Did He Die?

The message of the cross . . . is the power of God.
1 CORINTHIANS 1:18

 We can never grasp the horror of human sin until we realize it caused the Son of God to be crucified. Not Pilate, not Judas, not the mob—but sin. The ravages of war and poverty, the wrenching pain of loneliness and rejection. The haunting cry of the orphan and widow, the dying gasps of the world's starving—these and a thousand other tragedies all bear witness to the fact that we live in a world poisoned by sin. And that is why Jesus died. The terrible, bitter cup of humanity's sin sent Him to the Cross. Jesus prayed in those last hours, "O, My Father, if it is possible, let this cup pass from Me; nevertheless, not as I will, but as You will" (Matt. 26:39). There was no other way. Why did He drink that awful cup? So you and I would not have to.

Sin is the second most powerful force in the universe, for it sent Jesus to the Cross. Only one force is greater—the love of God.

Risen and Returning

*This same Jesus . . . will so come
in like manner as you saw Him go.*

ACTS 1:11

The resurrection of Jesus Christ is the key to God's plan for the future. Unless Christ was raised from the dead, there can be no future kingdom and no returning King. Unless Christ was raised from the dead, sin and death still reign, and God's plan of redemption remains unfulfilled. But Christ *has* been raised!

As the disciples stood watching after Jesus ascended into the heavens, the angels assured them that the risen Christ would some day be the returning Christ. "Men of Galilee, why do you stand gazing up into heaven? This same Jesus, who was taken up from you into heaven, will so come in like manner as you saw Him go into heaven" (Acts 1:11).

Just as surely as Christ rose from the dead, so He will return and take us to Himself. Every promise—without exception—will be fulfilled.

A Treasury of Faith

Perfect in Weakness

When I am weak, then I am strong.

2 CORINTHIANS 12:10

God's idea of strength and man's idea of strength are opposite one another. The Lord told Paul, "My strength is made perfect in weakness" (2 Cor. 12:9). Having learned this lesson, Paul could then say, "When I am weak, then I am strong" (2 Cor. 12:10). A paradox? Not really. Only when Paul admitted his own weakness and was willing to get out of the way, could God take over and work.

If we try to do God's will in our own strength, then we can take the credit for whatever gets accomplished. But that isn't God's way! When we let His strength work through us, then He alone will get the glory—and that is as it should be.

In the Old Testament God repeatedly told the leaders of Israel to reduce the size of their armies, or He announced in advance how their victory would be won. Why? So they would place their trust in Him and not in their own strength. As someone has said, "God's work, done in God's way, will never lack for God's provision."

A Treasury of Faith

True Thanksgiving

Oh, give thanks to the LORD, for He is good!

PSALM 107:1

Separated from friends, unjustly accused, brutally treated—if any man had a right to complain it was this man, languishing almost forgotten in a harsh Roman prison. But instead of complaints, his lips rang with words of praise and thanksgiving!

This was the apostle Paul—a man who had learned the meaning of true thanksgiving, even in the midst of great adversity. Look carefully at what he wrote during that prison experience: "Sing and make music in your heart to the Lord, always giving thanks to God the Father for everything, in the name of our Lord Jesus Christ" (Eph. 5:19–20, NIV).

Think of it! "Always giving thanks . . . for everything" no matter the circumstances. His guards and fellow prisoners must have thought him crazy—but that didn't stop him. Thanksgiving for Paul was not a once-a-year celebration, but a daily reality that made him a joyful person in every situation. May that be true of us.

A Treasury of Faith

In Tune with the Master

You shall surround me
with songs of deliverance.

PSALM 32:7

Out West an old sheepherder had a violin, but it was out of tune. He had no way of tuning it, so in desperation he wrote to one of the radio stations and asked them at a certain hour on a certain day to strike the tone "A." The officials of the station decided they would accommodate the old fellow, and on that particular day the true tone of "A" was broadcast. His fiddle was thus tuned, and once more his cabin echoed with joyful music. When we live apart from God, our lives get out of tune—out of harmony with others and with God. But if we live in tune with the Master, we, too, will find ourselves surrounded by His beautiful music.

As this new year begins, ask God to help you tune your life every day to His Word, so you can bring harmony and joy to those around you.

A Treasury of Faith

Christ Is Risen

He is not here, but is risen!

LUKE 24:6

Easter Sunday is the most triumphant and joyous day in the calendar of the Christian Church—and it should be!

For many people the resurrection of Jesus Christ is symbolized by new Easter clothes, or the bright color of daffodils and beautiful, white Easter lilies. But most of all, the wonder of His resurrection is symbolized in the hope that beats in the hearts of believers everywhere as they sing triumphantly: "Christ the Lord is risen today."

It is the message "Jesus is alive!" that lifts Christianity out of the category of dead superstitions and archaic religions and makes it the abiding faith of millions. The angel's message is true: "He is not here, but is risen!" And now God's promise is for you: "If you confess with your mouth the Lord Jesus and believe in your heart that God has raised Him from the dead, you will be saved" (Rom. 10:9).

A Treasury of Faith

God Wants Our Fellowship

Come near to God and he will come near to you.

JAMES 4:8, NIV

What a blessed promise and provision this is! It means each of us can come close to God, with the assurance He will come close to us— so close that we become conscious of His presence.
This is the greatest experience we can know.

But for most of us this isn't easy. Life presents us with too many distractions, and the last thing we have time for is to be alone with God. Children, work, television, the Internet, even church activities drain away our time. Maybe you will have to readjust your priorities. Maybe you will have to say "No" to certain activities or demands. Whatever it takes, make time to be alone with God.

Remember: He *wants* your fellowship, and He has done everything possible to make it a reality. He has forgiven your sins, at the cost of His own dear Son. He has given you His Word, and the priceless privilege of prayer and worship. He *will* come near to you, if you will come near to Him.

Peace, Perfect Peace

I will give you assured peace in this place.

JEREMIAH 14:13

"Worry," says Vance Havner, "is like sitting in a rocking chair. It will give you something to do, but it won't get you anywhere." Worry and anxiety have hounded the human race since the beginning of time, and modern man with all his innovations has not found the cure for the plague of worry. What is the answer? Imagine in your mind a ferocious ocean storm beating against a rocky shore. The lightning flashes, the thunder roars, the waves lash the rocks. But then imagine that you see a crevice in the rocky cliff—and inside is a little bird, its head serenely tucked under its wing, fast asleep. It knows the rock will protect it, and thus it sleeps in peace.

God promised Moses, "I will put you in the cleft of the rock, and will cover you with My hand" (Exod. 33:22). That is God's promise to us. Christ is our Rock, and we are secure in His hands forever. The storm rages, but our hearts are at rest.

A Treasury of Faith

God Cares for You

God is not the author of confusion but of peace.
1 CORINTHIANS 14:33

Who of us has not asked in times of affliction and difficulty—does God care for me? The Psalmist said, "Refuge failed me; no man cared for my soul" (Ps. 142:4 KJV). Martha, over-concerned with her workaday duties, said to Jesus, "Lord, do You not care?" How many faithful, loving mothers, overwhelmed by the burdens of motherhood, have cried anxiously, "Lord, do You not care?"

That question is forever answered in those reassuring words of Peter: "He cares for you" (1 Pet. 5:7). This is the Word of God. Even if the world passes away it will not change. You can be confident God cares for you. If He didn't, would He have sent Christ into the world to die for you? Of course not! That is why you can always turn to Him for the strength and encouragement you need.

Yes, life can be overwhelming at times. But when it is, remember this: God knows what you are facing, and "He cares for you."

A Treasury of Faith

Redeemed by Love

You were redeemed . . . with the precious blood of Christ.
1 PETER 1:18–19, NIV

The word *redeem* means to "buy back"—to recover by paying a price. The word *redeemed* can be illustrated from the ancient world by the position of a slave who had been captured in battle or enticed into serving one who was not his legal master. His real master, however, intent on recovering his slave's service and love, would buy him back—redeem him from the enemy—at great personal cost.

That is what God did for us. Captured by Satan and enticed into his service, we were slaves of sin, without any hope of deliverance. But God still loved us, and He was determined to restore us to His household. By His death on the Cross, Jesus paid the price for our deliverance, a price far greater than our true value. He did it solely because He loved us. Now we have been redeemed!

A Treasury of Faith

Unload Your Distress

Casting all your care upon Him,
for He cares for you.

1 PETER 5:7

I've been told that the French translation of this phrase, "Cast all your care upon Him" is "Unload your distresses upon God." Have you ever seen a dump truck get rid of its load? The driver simply pushes a button or pulls on a lever and the heavy load is discharged at the pre-scribed spot. The truck would be of no use if it carried its burden forever.

We were never meant to be crushed under the weight of care. We can push the button of faith or pull the lever of trust, and our burden is discharged upon the shoulder of Him who said He would gladly bear it. Unload the anxieties of the present moment upon Him, for He cares for you. If He loved you enough to take away the burden of your sins, can't you trust Him to take away every lesser burden as well?

A Treasury of Faith

A Victorious Christian

The Spirit also helps in our weaknesses. ROMANS 8:26

We need to rely constantly on the Holy Spirit. We need to remember that Christ dwells in us through the Holy Spirit. Our bodies are the dwelling place of the Third Person of the Trinity. Why don't we rely on Him as we should? We don't realize how weak we are. We don't realize how strong our enemy is. We may even doubt if God is really going to help us. Or we think we can do it all ourselves—or that we must. But we should ask Him to do it all and to take over in our lives. We should tell Him how weak, helpless, unstable, and unreliable we are. It is important that we stand aside and let Him take over in all our choices and decisions. We know that the Holy Spirit prays for us (Rom. 8:26), and what a comfort that should be to the weakest of us.

A victorious Christian is one who, in spite of worries, inner conflicts, and tensions, is confident that God is in control and will be victorious in the end. Whatever our difficulties, whatever our circumstances, we must remember, as Corrie ten Boom used to say, "Jesus is victor!"

A Treasury of Faith

It Was Love

I have loved you with an everlasting love;
therefore with lovingkindness I have drawn you.

JEREMIAH 31:3

Many people have difficulty believing God is a God of love. "How could He be," they ask, "when the world is filled with so much suffering and evil?" It is not an easy issue—but if you really want to know the reality of God's love, look at the Cross. It was love, divine love, that made Christ endure the Cross, despising the shame. It was love that restrained Him when He was falsely accused of blasphemy and led to Golgotha to die with common thieves. He raised not a hand against His enemies. It was love that kept Him from calling legions of angels to come to His defense. It was love that made Him, in a moment of agonizing pain, pause and give hope to a repentant sinner who cried, "Lord, remember me when You come into Your kingdom" (Luke 23:42).

It was love that caused Jesus to lift His voice and pray, "Father, forgive them, for they do not know what they do" (Luke 23:34). Does God love us? Yes—and the proof is the Cross.

A Treasury of Faith

Boundless Blessings

He gathers the lambs in his arms
and carries them close to his heart.

ISAIAH 40:11, NIV

🐑 The Old Testament gives a wonderful picture of God as our Shepherd. One Psalm begins, "Hear us, O Shepherd of Israel, you who lead Joseph like a flock" (Ps. 80:1, NIV). The almighty Creator of the universe stoops to be the Shepherd of His people! A shepherd protects and feeds his sheep, and pursues them when they stray. At evening he brings them into the fold, secure against every enemy. Without the shepherd, the sheep would scatter and wander into danger.

In the best-known of all Psalms, David makes the relationship personal. "The Lord is my shepherd," he cries exultantly, "I shall lack nothing." He then tells of God's constant care, until that day when "I will dwell in the house of the LORD forever" (Ps. 23:1, NIV). But the New Testament tells of another Shepherd—the Lord Jesus Christ: "I am the good shepherd. The good shepherd gives His life for the sheep" (John 10:11). He guides and protects us, and even gave His life so we will be safely in His fold forever.

A Treasury of Faith

"Come Home"

Our citizenship is in heaven,
from which we also eagerly wait for the Savior.
PHILIPPIANS 3:20

Once there was a widow and her son who lived in a miserable attic. Years before, she had married against her parents' wishes and had gone with her husband to live in a foreign land. He had proved irresponsible and unfaithful, and after a few years he died without having made any provision for her and the child. It was with the utmost difficulty that she managed to scrape together the bare necessities of life.

One day the postman knocked at the attic door. The mother recognized the handwriting on the letter he brought and with trembling fingers broke the seal. There was a check and a slip of paper with just two words: "Come home." Some day a similar experience will be ours—an experience shared by all who know Christ. We do not know when the call will come. It may be when we are in the midst of our work. It may be after weeks or months of illness. But some day a loving hand will be laid upon our shoulder and this brief message will be given: "Come home."

Patience and Prayer

We . . . do not cease to pray for you.

COLOSSIANS 1:9

Some years ago, a woman wrote me that she had pleaded for ten years for the conversion of her husband, but that he was more hardened than ever. I advised her to continue to plead. Sometime later I heard from her again. She said her husband was gloriously and miraculously converted in the eleventh year of her prayer vigil. How thankful she was that she had kept on praying!

The Scripture says, "Pray without ceasing" (1 Thess. 5:17). This should be the motto of every true follower of Jesus Christ. Never stop praying, no matter how dark and hopeless your case may seem. Your responsibility isn't to tell God *when* He must act or even *how* He must act. Your responsibility is simply to "pray without ceasing," trusting Him to act according to His perfect will.

A Treasury of Faith

Not Faith but Sight

The Son of man will come in the glory of His Father with His angels.
MATTHEW 16:27

Today Christ is hidden from our view (although through the Holy Spirit He lives in our hearts). Today is the day of faith; as Paul wrote, "We walk by faith, not by sight" (2 Cor. 5:7). Only in the future will we "see Him as He is" (1 John 3:2).

Christ's first appearing was quiet, almost unnoticed—a humble manger, simple shepherds, an insignificant corner of the Roman Empire. His second appearing will be glorious and universal. He will be accompanied by His angels and will defeat every enemy until He subdues the whole earth.

How easily the events of the moment crowd out the promise of eternity! The present seems so real; the unseen future seems so illusory. But in reality the opposite is true. Don't let the present consume you. Instead, "seek those things which are above, where Christ is" (Col. 3:1).

A Treasury of Faith

The Light of God's Love

O LORD my God, You are very great; . . .
You who laid the foundations of the earth.

PSALM 104:1, 5

God's love did not begin at Calvary. Before the morning stars sang together, before the world was baptized with the first light, before the first blades of tender grass peeped out, God was love. Turn back to the unwritten pages of countless eons before God spoke this present earth into existence, when the earth was "without form and void" and the deep, silent darkness of space stood in stark contrast to the brilliance of God's glory and His cherubim and seraphim.

Even then, God was love. Before the worlds were created, He knew all about us and the need we would have some day for Christ to die for us. So in His love "he chose us in him before the creation of the world" (Eph. 1:4, NIV). God does not change—and neither does His love. He loved you before you were born . . . He loves you now . . . and He will love you forever. Will you love Him in return?

A Treasury of Faith

Refined and Purified

When He has tested me, I shall come forth as gold.

JOB 23:10

 Affliction can be a means of refining and of purification. Just as ore must pass through the refiner's furnace before it can yield up its gold, so our lives must sometimes pass through God's furnace of affliction before they can bring forth something beautiful and useful to Him. We might never have had the songs of Fanny Crosby had she not been afflicted with blindness. George Matheson would never have given the world his immortal song, "O Love That Wilt Not Let Me Go," had it not been for the pain of personal tragedy and heartache. The "Hallelujah Chorus" was written by Handel when he was poverty-stricken and suffering from a paralyzed right side and right arm.

Affliction can also make us stronger in our faith and develop our confidence in God's watch care over us. It may also drive us back to the right path when we have wandered. David said, "Before I was afflicted I went astray, but now I keep your word" (Ps. 119:67). Whatever the reason, if God sends affliction your way, take it in faith as a blessing not a curse.

Peril of Preoccupation

Behold, God is great, and we do not know Him.

JOB 36:26

One evening in Jerusalem I looked out my hotel window and saw the lights of Bethlehem in the distance. I thought about the response of the innkeeper when Mary and Joseph wanted to find a room where the Child could be born. The innkeeper was not hostile; he was not opposed to them but his inn was crowded, his hands were full, and his mind was preoccupied. Perhaps he told them, "I wish I could help you, but I must keep my priorities. After all, this is a business, and this coming Child is no real concern of mine. But I'm not a hardhearted man. Over there is the stable. You are welcome to use it if you care to. That is the best I can do. Now I must get back to my work. My guests need me."

And this is the answer that millions give today. It is the answer of preoccupation—not fierce opposition, not furious hatred, but unconcern about spiritual things. We are simply too preoccupied with other things to welcome Christ into our lives. Don't let that happen to you!

A Treasury of Faith

Pure in Heart

Blessed are the pure in heart,
for they shall see God.

Matthew 5:8

Why does Jesus say we should be "pure *in heart*"? The reason is because our heart—our inner being—is the root of all our actions. From our hearts come our motives, our desires, our goals, our emotions. If our hearts aren't right, neither will be our actions. Jesus put it this way: "From within, out of the heart of men, proceed evil thoughts, adulteries, fornications, murders, thefts, covetousness, wickedness, deceit, lewdness, an evil eye, blasphemy, pride, foolishness" (Mark 7:21–22). Not a very pretty picture! But God wants to give us a pure heart—and He will. He does this first of all when we turn to Christ in repentance and faith, for "the blood of Jesus Christ His Son cleanses us from all sin" (1 John 1:7). But He does it also day by day, as we submit to the Holy Spirit and—with His help—flee from evil and seek what is good. "Blessed are the pure *in heart*."

God Is Our Strength

The LORD is my light and my salvation; whom shall I fear?

PSALM 27:1

It is a *fact* that the Lord is my light and my salvation. So why should I be afraid? Since the Lord fears nothing, why should we fear?

The Scripture also declares that God is a "very present help in trouble" (Ps. 46:1). If we can't trust the all-powerful, all-knowing, all-loving God of the universe to help us, where can we turn? But we *can* trust Him! God is able, indeed He is anxious, to deliver us from all sorts of trouble. He wants to give us strength to overcome the temptation to sin that separates Him from those He loves. He wants to give us the courage to confront our problems (instead of avoiding them or denying them), and then to find the practical wisdom and help we need to deal with them.

What do you fear today? Failure? Rejection? An illness or physical danger? The uncertainty of the future? Whatever it is, ask God to help you turn it over to Him. "The LORD is my light and my salvation; whom shall I fear?"

A Treasury of Faith

The Good Shepherd

The good shepherd lays down his life for the sheep.

JOHN 10:11, NIV

One of the figures of speech Jesus applied to Himself was that of a shepherd. He said, "I am the good shepherd. The good shepherd lays down his life for the sheep. The hired hand is not the shepherd who owns the sheep. . . . I know my sheep and my sheep know me" (John 10:11–14, NIV). Note four things about Jesus, the Good Shepherd. He *owns* the sheep; they belong to Him. Next, He *guards* the sheep; He never abandons them when danger approaches. Also, He *knows* the sheep; He calls them by name and they follow Him. Finally, He *lays down His life* for the sheep; their salvation is His primary concern.

The Bible says, "We are His people and the sheep of His pasture" (Ps. 100:3). Because we belong to Christ, we can be secure and at rest.

A Treasury of Faith

Complete Consecration

Whoever desires to come after Me, let him deny himself.

MARK 8:34

Today Christ is calling Christians to cleansing—to dedication—to consecration—to full surrender. If you are a Christian and have been suffering defeat or have been living outside the will of God, I beg you to surrender every area of your life to Christ. Only surrendered Christians will make an impact on our world. The world does not need any more lukewarm Christians, or lazy Christians, or quarrelsome Christians, or doubting Christians, or prideful Christians. The Bible says, "a double minded man is unstable in all his ways" (James 1:8, KJV). What keeps you from a full surrender of your life to the King of kings and the Lord of lords?

Your response will make the difference between success and failure in your spiritual life. It will make the difference between your needing help and being able to help others. It will revolutionize your habits, your prayer life, your Bible reading, your giving, your testimony, and your church relationship. This is the Christian's hour of decision!

A Treasury of Faith

And though this world, with devils filled,
should threaten to undo us,
We will not fear, for God hath willed
His truth to triumph through us.

A Mighty Fortress

He is my refuge and my fortress;
my God, in Him I will trust.

PSALM 91:2

A refuge is a place safely out of harm's way. A fortress is a fortified
building that is virtually impenetrable by conventional means.
Martin Luther wrote a wonderful hymn that says, "A mighty
fortress is our God; a bulwark never failing. Our helper He amidst
the flood; of mortal ills prevailing." What a statement about the
magnificent power and protection of God!

Does God care for you and me? Can we turn to Him in trust and
faith when troubles and temptations threaten to overwhelm us? Yes—
a thousand times yes! What greater proof do we need than that He
sent His Son, Jesus Christ, to die in our place?

A Treasury of Faith

In the Presence of Christ

The upright shall dwell in your presence.

PSALM 140:13

What would you do if you were about to meet the Queen of England? I'm sure you would go out of your way to dress correctly and to be properly briefed so you didn't say the wrong thing or act in an improper way.

Some day you and I will meet a far greater Sovereign: The King of the universe. His dazzling glory far exceeds that of any earthly monarch, and in His presence we can only bow in humble worship and praise. Our cry will be that of Revelation: "You are worthy, O Lord, to receive glory and honor and power" (Rev. 4:11).

Are you prepared for that day when you will meet the King of kings face to face? No one knows the day or the hour when life will end. The time for you to prepare is now, by committing your life to Christ and beginning to live as a child of the King

A Treasury of Faith

Abiding Peace

Fear not, for I am with you; be not dismayed, for I am your God.
ISAIAH 41:10

Whenever I think of God's faithfulness in the midst of suffering
I am reminded of my dear late friend Corrie ten Boom, the remarkable
Dutch woman who (with her family) hid Jews from the Nazis. After being
imprisoned in Ravensbruk, the infamous concentration camp, Corrie
traveled the world telling her story of suffering, forgiveness, and joy.

For thirty-five years she never had a permanent home, but when she was
eighty-five and in declining health, some friends provided her with a
lovely house in California. It was a luxury she never dreamed she would
have (and one she never would have pursued on her own).

One day her friend, the late movie director James Collier, was
visiting. He said, "Corrie, hasn't God been good to give you this
beautiful house?" She replied firmly, "Jimmy, God was good when I was
in Ravensbruk, too!" Most of us will never experience the horrors Corrie
knew. But no matter what we face, we can depend on God's promise:
"Fear not; for I am with you."

A Treasury of Faith

Our Loving, Compassionate God

I am the bread of life.

JOHN 6:35

Jesus came to the world so we could know, once and for all, that God is concerned about the way we live, the way we believe, and the way we die. God could have told us in other ways, of course—and He had, throughout the pages of the Old Testament and in the lives of His people. By His written Word He declared His love.

But Jesus was the Living Word. By His life, death, and resurrection, Jesus *demonstrated* God's love in a way we could never deny. Paul wrote, "But God demonstrates His own love toward us, in that while we were still sinners, Christ died for us" (Rom. 5:8).

Every time He fed the hungry, He was saying, "I am the bread of life." Every time He healed a suffering person, He was saying, "It hurts Me to see you in pain." Every move He made, every miracle He performed, every word He spoke was for the purpose of reconciling a lost world to the loving, compassionate God.

God's Hand of Blessing

Every good gift and every perfect gift is from above.

JAMES 1:17

In the midst of the Lord's Prayer are these familiar words: "Give us this day our daily bread" (Matt. 6:11). They remind us that we are dependent on God for everything, and He is the giver of every blessing. "Every good gift and every perfect gift is from above, and comes down from the Father of lights" (James 1:17).

Some people say, "Why should I pray for my daily bread? I can take care of my own needs!" But listen: If it weren't for God's love and grace, you wouldn't have anything. We need to pray this prayer every day, because we need to be reminded to trust God in everything.

This prayer reminds us also of Jesus' words: "I am the bread of life. He who comes to Me shall never hunger" (John 6:35). Thank God for all His gifts—especially Christ, the greatest gift of all.

Triumph Through Trust

Neither death nor life, . . . nor things present nor things to come, . . .
shall be able to separate us from the love of God.

ROMANS 8:38-39

There are two ways to respond to adversity: discouragement or trust. The problem with giving in to discouragement is that it only makes things worse, for with it may come bitterness, anger, jealousy, revenge, and so forth. We may even try to escape through drugs or alcohol. But do *any* of these solve the problem? No! God has a better way—the way of trust. Sometimes He may show us that we were in the wrong. When that is the case, we need to confess it, repent, and seek His forgiveness. Sometimes, however, we can only accept what is happening and ask God to help us endure it and triumph over it.

One of the best ways to overcome adversity, I've found, is to praise God right in the middle of the turmoil. Turning to God's Word will also encourage us; many of the Psalms, for example, were written in the midst of suffering and adversity. Follow the Psalmist's example: "Bless the LORD, O my soul, and forget not all His benefits" (Ps. 103:2).

A Treasury of Faith

God's True Purposes

Whatever you ask in My name,
that I will do. . . .

JOHN 14:13

Prayer links us with God's true purposes, for us and for the world.
It not only brings the blessings of God's will to our own personal lives,
it brings us the added blessing of being in step with God's plan. Prayer
also—in ways we will never fully understand this side of eternity—
makes us partners with God in what He is doing in the world.
God works through our prayers!

The model prayer Jesus has given us concludes with, "Thine is
the kingdom, and the power, and the glory for ever" (Matt. 6:13, KJV).
Remember, too, that we must seek God's glory in our prayers and not
just our own selfish desires. If we are to have our prayers answered, we
must be willing to give God the glory when He acts—no matter what
the result. Our Lord said to His disciples, "Whatever you ask
in My name, that I will do, that the Father may be glorified
in the Son" (John 14:13).

A Treasury of Faith

He Suffered for You

His visage was marred more than any man.

ISAIAH 52:14

When Jesus Christ was on the Cross, His blood draining the life from His body, He knew what it was like to be alone and wracked with pain. But Jesus' pain was far more than just physical pain, for He was suffering God's judgment on all the sins of the ages—the greatest darkness of the soul ever known. As the divine Son of God, He was perfect and without sin. But all our sins were placed on Him, and He took the judgment and Hell we alone deserve. He died in our place.

Why did Jesus suffer? For you. For me. That we might have eternal life and have His peace in the midst of life's storms. That we might know that He understands our pain and suffering and stands ready to help.

Why did Jesus suffer? Because God loves us. Because God loves *you*, and Christ willingly went to the Cross for *you*. There was no other way for sin's penalty to be paid, and for us to be redeemed. The Cross is the measure of God's love. How will *you* respond to His love, poured out on the Cross for *you?*

A Treasury of Faith

The Spirit of God

I will pray the Father, and He will give you another Helper,
that He may abide with you forever.

JOHN 14:16

During His lifetime on earth, Christ's presence could be experienced only by a small group of people at any given time. Now Christ dwells through the Spirit in the hearts of all who have received Him as Savior and Lord. The Apostle Paul wrote, "Do you not know . . . that the Spirit of God dwells in you?" (1 Cor. 3:16). The Holy Spirit is given to every believer—not for a limited time, but forever. If He left us for one moment, we would be in deep trouble.

But He doesn't! He is there to give you both the gifts and the power to work for Christ. He is there to give you strength in the moment of temptation. He is there to produce the fruit of "love, joy, peace, longsuffering, kindness, goodness, faithfulness, gentleness, self-control" (Gal. 5:22–23).

You will never have more of the Holy Spirit than you do right now. But will He have more of you?

A Treasury of Faith

Trust and Obey

Blessed is the man who makes the LORD his trust.

PSALM 40:4, NIV

Some years ago someone gave my little boy a dollar. He brought it to me and said, "Daddy, keep this for me." But in a few minutes he came back and said, "Daddy, I'd better keep my own dollar." He tucked it in his pocket and went out to play. In a few minutes he came back with tears in his eyes, saying, "Daddy, I lost my dollar. Help me find it."

How often we commit our burdens to the Lord and then fail to trust Him by taking matters into our own hands. Then, when we have messed things up, we pray, "Oh, Lord, help me, I'm in trouble."

The choice is yours. Do you want to trust your life in God's "pocket" or keep it in your own? The Bible's promise is true: "Blessed is the man who makes the LORD his trust."

A Treasury of Faith

Our Infinite God

Great is the LORD, and greatly to be praised.

PSALM 48:1

As a boy I grew up in the rural American South. My idea of the ocean was so small that the first time I saw the Atlantic I couldn't comprehend how any lake could be so big! The vastness of the ocean cannot be understood until it is seen.

This is the same with God's love. It passes knowledge. Until you actually experience it, no one can describe its wonders to you. The opening lines of one of our great old hymns declare, "O the deep, deep love of Jesus / Vast, unmeasured, boundless, free! / Rolling as a mighty ocean / In its fullness over me." Behind the love of God lies His omniscience—His ability to "know and understand all." Omniscience is a quality of God that is His alone. God possesses infinite knowledge and an awareness that is uniquely His. At all times, even in the midst of any type of suffering, I can realize that He knows, loves, watches, understands, and, more than that, has a purpose.

No matter what comes your way . . . no matter how tempted you are to give in to despair . . . never forget: God's love for you can never be exhausted, for His love is beyond measure.

A Treasury of Faith

Look to God

Lift up your heads, because your redemption draws near.
LUKE 21:28

If you've ever flown in an airplane you know that your perspective of the earth is far different from what it was when you were on the ground. Pictures of the earth that have been taken from the moon and from space show an earth that looks much different from what we see down here.

This is the kind of perspective God wants to give us concerning our lives. As we look to God, instead of to ourselves and our circumstances, our perspectives change. Don't get bogged down in the circumstances of life. At the moment we see only our immediate problems and burdens, but God sees the whole. He sees not only the present, but the future as well. He wants to lift us above ourselves. He wants us to see everything in light of His plans. The Psalmist said, "The LORD will perfect that which concerns me" (Ps. 138:8).

Don't get bogged down. Keep your eyes on God, for He sees the whole picture, and He knows what is best for you. You can trust Him, because He loves you.

A Treasury of Faith

God's Perfect Plan

*Be transformed . . . that you may prove what is that . . .
perfect will of God.*

ROMANS 12:2

The Bible reveals that God has a plan for every life, and that if we
live in constant fellowship with Him, He will direct and lead us in
the fulfillment of this plan.

God does not reveal His plan through fortune-tellers, astrologers,
soothsayers, and workers of hocus-pocus. His perfect will is reserved for
those who have trusted Christ for salvation. He shares His secrets only
with those who are redeemed and transformed, and who humbly seek
His will for their lives.

You cannot know the will of God for your life unless you first come
to the cross and confess that you are a sinner and receive Christ as Lord
and Savior. Once you do come to Him, you begin a whole new life—life
not lived for yourself but for Christ. From that moment on God wants
to show you His will. Whatever decisions you face today, commit them
to God and ask Him to guide you—and He will.

A Treasury of Faith

Peace with God

Let the peace of God rule in your hearts.
COLOSSIANS 3:15

Science has confirmed what the Bible taught centuries ago: There is a close relationship between our minds and bodies. Proverbs puts it this way: "A cheerful heart is good medicine, but a crushed spirit dries up the bones" (Prov. 17:22, NIV).

But there is also a close relationship between our mental and physical health and the health of our spiritual lives. Guilt, fear, jealousy, bitterness, futility, escapism—these and a host of other problems are spiritual ills, brought about by the disease of sin. Like poison, they can sicken us in mind and body.

But when Christ comes into our lives, He removes our guilt and takes away our fears. He gives us love for others and a new purpose in life. His joy and peace neutralize sin's poison—and that promotes emotional and physical health. Does that mean our emotional and physical problems will vanish? Not necessarily. But like a spring of pure water, God's peace in our hearts brings cleansing and refreshment to our minds and bodies.

A Treasury of Faith

Infinite Grace

Grace and truth came through Jesus Christ.

JOHN 1:17

The word *grace* means more than just God's kindness or gentleness toward us, or even His mercy. It means His undeserved favor. It means God owes nothing to us, and we deserve nothing from Him. When the Bible says "by grace you have been saved" (Eph. 2:5), it means our salvation was totally unmerited. It came solely because of God's grace.

The *motive* of grace is the infinite, compassionate love of a merciful God, but the *work* of grace was Christ's death on the Cross. When I imagine Christ hanging from the Cross, the spikes in His hands, the crown of thorns on His brow, His blood draining from His body, the soldiers mocking Him—then I begin to see the depth of God's grace. Then I know that nothing can equal the infinite love of God for a sinful world.

But God's grace is also exhibited when we humbly bow before Christ in repentance and faith, for then we find forgiveness. Thank God for His grace, for without it we would have no hope!

A Treasury of Faith

The Triumphs of Grace

I, even I, am He who blots out your transgressions. . . .

ISAIAH 43:25

When Charles Wesley experienced the joy of divine forgiveness, he told a Moravian friend of his new sense of pardon, and added, "I suppose I had better keep silent about it." "Oh, no, my brother," came the reply. "If you had a thousand tongues, you should go and use them all for Jesus."

Charles Wesley went home and wrote the great hymn: "Oh for a thousand tongues to sing / My great Redeemer's praise, / The glories of my God and King, / The triumphs of His grace!"

To a burdened, benighted world, crushed under the weight of its own wickedness, God says, "I, even I, am He who blots out your transgressions" (Isa. 43:25). This is glorious news, and it applies to all people everywhere—including you. Have you received God's gift of forgiveness? If you have, thank Him for it—and if not, by faith invite Christ into your life today.

A Treasury of Faith

A Home in Heaven

If I go and prepare a place for you,
I will come again and receive you to Myself.

JOHN 14:3

During Christ's ministry on earth He had no permanent home. He once said, "Foxes have holes and birds of the air have nests, but the Son of Man has no place to lay his head" (Matt. 8:20, NIV).

What a contrast to the home He left in order to come to earth—His Heavenly home. From all eternity His dwelling place had been filled with unimaginable glory and splendor. And yet, the Bible says, He "emptied Himself . . . being born in human likeness" (Phil. 2:7, NRSV). Out of love for you and me, He left Heaven's glory for earth's misery.

But the story doesn't end there. Now He has returned to Heaven—and some day we will join Him. Think of it. He wants to share Heaven's glory with us! One evening a little girl was taking a walk with her father. Looking up at the stars she exclaimed, "Daddy, if the wrong side of heaven is so beautiful, what must the right side be like!"

A Treasury of Faith

Pray Without Ceasing

Men always ought to pray and not lose heart.

LUKE 18:1

A prayer does not have to be eloquent or contain the language and terms of a theologian. In fact, sometimes our simplest, most heartfelt prayers are the most pleasing to God.

When you made your decision for Christ, you became a child of God, adopted by Him into His family forever. Now you have the wonderful privilege of coming directly into His presence and addressing God as your Father. In the beginning you may not be fluent, but it's important to begin. My wife has a notebook she has kept of our children as they were beginning to talk. She treasures these first attempts, mistakes and all. She said, "I wouldn't take anything for that book."

When Paul said we should "pray without ceasing" (1 Thess. 5:17) he chose a term used in his day to describe a persistent cough. Repeatedly, throughout our day, we should be turning quickly to God to praise and thank Him, and to ask for His help. God is interested in everything we do, and nothing is too great or too insignificant to share with Him.

A Treasury of Faith

The Victorious Chime

I, even I, am the LORD, and besides Me there is no savior.

ISAIAH 43:11

It is said that during Napoleon's Austrian campaign his army advanced to within six miles of the town of Feldkirch. It looked as though his men would take it without resistance. But as Napoleon's army advanced toward their objective in the night, the Christians of Feldkirch gathered in their little church to pray.
It was Easter eve.

The next morning at sunrise the bells of the village pealed out across the countryside. Napoleon's army, not realizing it was Easter Sunday, thought that in the night the Austrian army had moved into Feldkirch and the bells were ringing in jubilation. Napoleon ordered a retreat, and the battle at Feldkirch never took place. The Easter bells caused the enemy to flee, and peace reigned in the Austrian countryside.

As Easter is celebrated each year, churches and cathedrals around the world will ring their bells—not to sound Christ's death knell but to declare Christ's victory over death. He is the risen Lord, and because of Him our final enemy—death—has been defeated and peace reigns in our hearts!

A Treasury of Faith

A Home in Heaven

You yourselves had {in heaven} a better and lasting possession.
HEBREWS 10.34, AB

Paul once wrote, "If only for this life we have hope in Christ, we are to be pitied more than all men" (1 Cor. 15:19, NIV). If there is no life after death, no Heaven, no promise of a better world—then life is empty, hopeless, without meaning or purpose. But this life is not all! Ahead is Heaven, and some day "we shall always be with the Lord" (1 Thess. 4:17). Some day we will go to a home where all is happiness, joy, and peace. How barren our lives would be if we didn't have this hope.

Knowing Heaven is real will make a difference in the way we live. For one thing, we won't become attached to the things of this world. We will say with Paul, "I have learned in whatever state I am, to be content" (Phil. 4:11). But Heaven should also give us a burden for those who do not have this hope. Every day you meet people who do not know Christ. Will you tell them?

A Treasury of Faith

The Knowledge of God

Oh, the depth of the riches both of the wisdom and knowledge of God!

ROMANS 11:33

It was the mystery of lightning (so the story goes) that prompted Benjamin Franklin to attach a key to the tail of a kite during a thunderstorm, to prove the identity of lightning and electricity. We have always tried to understand the world around us; it is one of the things that sets us apart from the animals. Some of the mysteries of the past have been fathomed by science. Others still puzzle us. This fact remains: All of the garnered wisdom of the ages is only a scratch on the surface of humanity's search for the knowledge of the universe.

This inability to comprehend fully the mysteries of God's creation does not in any way cast doubt on the Christian faith. On the contrary, it enhances our belief. We do not understand the intricate patterns of the stars in their courses, but we know that He who created them does, and that just as surely as He guides them, He is charting a safe course for us.

The next time you look into the heavens at night, remember the words of the Psalmist: "The heavens declare the glory of God" (Ps. 19:1).

A Treasury of Faith

God Controls the Clock

There is laid up for me the crown of righteousness.

2 TIMOTHY 4:8

Many people are asking, "Where is history heading?" A careful student of the Bible will see that God controls the clock of destiny. Amidst the world's confusion, God's omnipotent hand moves, working out His unchanging plan and purpose.

Not that we always see His hand at work. As the old English hymn writer William Cowper put it, "God moves in a mysterious way, His wonders to perform." God is not absent. By His providence He sustains us, and behind the scenes He is working to bring about His divine purpose.

What is that purpose? Paul recorded it this way: "That . . . He might gather together in one all things in Christ, both which are in heaven and which are on earth" (Eph. 1:10). Some day Satan's rule will be ended, and Christ will reign as Lord over all creation. Some day all the sin and rebellion of this corrupted universe will be destroyed, and Christ's kingdom of righteousness and peace will rule forever. Don't be discouraged by what you see in the headlines every day. God is at work, and some day Christ will rule.

A Treasury of Faith

Pray Anywhere, Any Time

Rejoice always, pray without ceasing.

1 THESSALONIANS 5:16-17

Prayer is an essential part of a healthy Christian life. Just as omitting an essential vitamin from our diet will make us physically weak, so a lack of prayer will make us spiritually anemic.

The Bible says, "Pray without ceasing." It isn't enough to get out of bed in the morning, quickly bow our head, and repeat a few sentences. Instead, we need to set aside specific times to be alone with God, speaking to Him in prayer and listening to Him speak through His Word. If you set aside special times for prayer, your unconscious mind will be saturated with prayer all day long.

For the overworked mother or other busy person this may seem impossible (although even a few minutes alone with God can reap rich rewards). But even when we are busy, we can "pray without ceasing" in our hearts and minds. We can pray anywhere, any time—and God will hear us. Today let prayer saturate your life "without ceasing."

The Future Life

*As for man, his days are like grass;
as a flower of the field, so he flourishes.*

PSALM 103:15

The Bible reminds us that our days are as grass. For a brief time we flourish, but soon we wither and die. Yet the minutes of our lives can be flecked with the gold of eternity. Instead of wasting them—as we so easily do—God exhorts us to redeem the time.

But our lives are also immortal. God made us different from the other creatures. He made us in His own image, a living soul. Don't let anyone tell you that we are simply a higher species of animal. If you believe that, you will begin to act like one. No! You are far greater.

One thousand years from this day you will be more alive than you are at this moment. The Bible teaches that life does not end at the cemetery. There is a future life with God for those who put their trust in His Son, Jesus Christ. Make sure of your relationship to Christ, and then ask God to help you live each day for His glory.

A Treasury of Faith

God's Holiness

Holy, holy, holy is the LORD of hosts;
the whole earth is full of His glory!

ISAIAH 6:3

The Bible teaches that God is absolutely holy and pure. From Genesis to Revelation, God reveals Himself as so holy He cannot even look on sin. Christ cried from the Cross, "My God, My God, why have You forsaken Me?" (Mark 15:34). What a horrible moment, as the blackness of human sin—now laid upon Christ—caused the Father to turn away in disgust. In that moment Jesus endured the ultimate punishment for our sins—the punishment of being banished from the presence of His Father on our behalf.

If you were asked to list the things you are thankful for, what would you include? Perhaps your family, health, friends, church—and those wouldn't be wrong. We should be grateful for every gift God gives us. But the greatest gift of all is the gift of His Son, who endured the penalty we deserved for our sin, so we could be reconciled to a holy God. Never take that gift for granted! "Thanks be to God for his indescribable gift!" (2 Cor. 9:15).

A Treasury of Faith

The King of Kings

A scepter of righteousness is the scepter of Your kingdom.

PSALM 45:6

From his very birth Christ was recognized as King. Something about him inspired allegiance, loyalty and homage. Wise men brought Him gifts. Shepherds fell down and worshiped Him. Herod, realizing that there is never room for two thrones in one kingdom, sought His life. As Jesus began His ministry, His claims upon people's lives were total and absolute. He allowed no divided loyalty. He demanded and received complete adoration and devotion. Mature men and women left their businesses and gave themselves in complete obedience to Him. Many of them gave their lives, pouring out the last full measure of devotion.

His words caused even His most avowed enemies to say, "No man ever spoke like this Man!" (John 7:46). And yet He was more than a poet, more than a statesman, more than a physician. We cannot understand Christ until we understand that He was the King of kings and the Lord of lords. Like Thomas, our only response must be to bow down and confess, "My Lord and my God!" (John 20:28).

A Treasury of Faith

God Promises Protection

I will never leave you nor forsake you.

HEBREWS 13:5

Never doubt that you are in the midst of a battle—a spiritual battle with Satan, who will do everything he can to discourage and defeat you. Never underestimate his determination or misunderstand his intentions. God wants to teach us how to defend ourselves against sin and Satan. Satan, the ultimate bully, attacks us at our weakest points and wants to defeat us so that we will not be effective for God.

God offers spiritual "training" to build us up inside in much the same way that physical exercise can build us up on the outside. He has also provided all the resources we need to defend ourselves and keep Satan at bay. These include the Bible, prayer, faith, righteous living, and the Holy Spirit within us.

But, like physical training, we must be diligent in their application. God has not promised to shield us from trouble, but He has promised to protect us in the midst of trouble. Most of all, never forget that because of Christ's death and resurrection, Satan is already a defeated foe—and some day the war will be over.

A Treasury of Faith

Faith Grows by Expression

You are the light of the world.

MATTHEW 5:14

Tom Allan, Scotland's famous preacher, was brought to Christ while a soldier was singing, "Were you there when they crucified my Lord?" He said it was neither the song nor the voice, but the spirit in which that soldier sang—something about his manner, something about his sincerity of expression—that convicted Allan of his wicked life and turned him to the Savior.

Jesus said, "You are the light of the world. . . . Let your light so shine before [others], that they may see your good works, and glorify your Father in heaven" (Matt. 5:14, 16).

Our faith becomes stronger as we express it; a growing faith is a sharing faith. Pray now for those you know who need Christ, and ask God to help you be a witness to them—by the life you live and the words you speak.

A Treasury of Faith

Beyond the Starry Sky

We are looking for the city that is to come.

HEBREWS 13:14, NRSV

Paul looked forward to death with great anticipation. He said, "For to me, to live is Christ, and to die is gain" (Phil. 1:21). Death for him was not an enemy to be feared, but a reality to be welcomed, in God's time. For him death was the joyous gateway to new life—the life of Heaven. Without the resurrection of Christ there could be no hope for the future. The Bible promises that someday we are going to stand face to face with the resurrected Christ. All our questions will be answered, and all our sorrows and fears will vanish. An old gospel hymn puts it well:

Face to face with Christ my Savior, face to face, what will it be?
When with rapture I behold Him, Jesus Christ who died for me?
Face to face I shall behold Him, far beyond the starry sky;
Face to face in all His glory I shall see Him by and by.

—*Carrie E. Breck*

We Can Count on Him

Blessed is the man whose strength is in You.

PSALM 84:5

Someone has written a little verse that goes:
Said the robin to the sparrow, I should really like to know,
Why these anxious human beings, rush about and worry so.
Said the sparrow to the robin, Friend, I think that it must be,
That they have no heavenly Father such as cares for you and me.

Jesus used the carefree attitude of the birds to underscore the fact that worrying is unnatural. "Look at the birds of the air, for they neither sow nor reap; . . . yet your heavenly Father feeds them" (Matt. 6:26). If He cares for tiny birds and frail flowers, why can't we count on Him for every aspect of our lives? After all, He loves us so much that He sent His Son into the world to save us.

We are that valuable to Him!

A Treasury of Faith

What a Friend we have in Jesus

All our sins and griefs to bear

What a privelege to carry

Everything to God in prayer

More Attached to God

God is our refuge and strength, an ever present help in trouble.

PSALM 46:1, NIV

A young Irishman, Joseph Scriven (1820- 1886), was deeply in love with a young woman, and their marriage plans had been made. The night before their wedding, however, she drowned in a tragic accident. For months Scriven was bitter, in utter despair. At last he turned to Christ, and through His grace, found peace and comfort. Out of this experience he wrote the familiar hymn that has brought consolation to millions of aching hearts: "What a friend we have in Jesus / All our sins and griefs to bear!"

Sometimes our way lies in the sunlight. It was so for Joseph Scriven as he approached his wedding day. But like him, we may find that our path also leads through the dark shadows of loss, disappointment, and sorrow. Yet even sorrows turn to blessings when they make us less attached to the earth and more attached to God. Then more than ever we discover that Jesus truly is our friend—
"All our sins and griefs to bear!"

A Treasury of Faith

Christ Is King

Your kingdom is an everlasting kingdom.

PSALM 145:13

The government in God's kingdom is unique. It is not a democracy where the people govern, but a "Christocracy" where Christ is the supreme authority. In a society of unredeemed people, democracy is the only fair and equitable system. But no democracy can ever be better than the people who make it up. When citizens are selfishly motivated, the government will be inequitable. When people are dishonest, the government will be the same. When everyone wants his own way, someone is going to get hurt.

But in God's kingdom, Christ is King. He is compassionate, fair, merciful, and just. When He is sovereign in men's hearts, anguish turns to peace, hatred is transformed into love, and misunderstanding into harmony. Is Christ the King of your motives and your attitudes?

A Treasury of Faith

A Prepared Place

In my Father's house are many mansions.

JOHN 14:2

As much as our homes mean to us, they are not permanent. Sometimes I look at my own adult children and can hardly believe they are all grown and on their own. The house that once rang with the laughter of children now seems empty. Those disciples who for Christ's sake gave up houses and lands and loved ones knew little of home life or home joys. It was as if Jesus were saying to them, "We have no lasting home here on earth, but my Father's house is a home where we will be together for all eternity."

The venerable Bishop Ryle is reputed to have said, "Heaven is a prepared place for a prepared people, and those who enter shall find that they are neither unknown or unexpected."

Even life's happiest experiences last but a moment, yet Heaven's joy is eternal. Some day we will go to our eternal Home—and Christ will be there to welcome us!

A Treasury of Faith

Rest for the Weary

Come to Me . . . and I will give you rest.
MATTHEW 11:28

We forget that Jesus was human as well as divine. He had calluses on His hands. If the chisel slipped and cut His finger, His blood was red and warm like ours. He knew what it meant to work long hours, to come in at night tired and weary. That is one of the reasons Jesus could say with such appeal, "Come to Me, all you who labor and are heavy laden, and I will give you rest" (Matt. 11:28).

When we are exhausted and hurting, we can take comfort from the fact that Jesus knows what it is to be exhausted and hurting also. But the greatest work Jesus did was not in the carpenter's shop, nor at the marriage feast in Cana where He turned the water into wine. The greatest work Jesus did was not when He made the blind to see, the deaf to hear, the dumb to speak, nor even the dead to rise.

What was His greatest work? His greatest work was what He accomplished through the Cross and Resurrection. There the burden of our sins was placed on Him, and there He won our salvation. And that is why we can come by faith to Him, and He will give us rest.

A Treasury of Faith

The Message of Easter

He has risen! He is not here.

MARK 16:6 NIV

The message of Easter is the central focus of Christianity. The Apostle Paul said, "If Christ has not been raised, your faith is futile; you are still in your sins" (1 Cor. 15:17, NIV). It is as simple as that. If Christ is still dead, then He cannot be our Savior, for He was not the Son of God, and He died like all men. More than that, Heaven's doors are still locked.

But if Christ is risen, as the Scriptures teach and as hundreds of witnesses testified (none of whom ever recanted that testimony despite threats and death for many of them), then we have the ultimate hope of humanity—eternal life with the God who made us and the certainty of life beyond the grave.

What does Easter mean to you? It should mean everything, because Christ has conquered death! And that makes all the difference—now and forever!

A Treasury of Faith

Full Surrender

Whoever loses his life for My sake . . .will save it.

MARK 8:35

A police sergeant once asked me the secret of victorious Christian living. I told him there is no magic formula. But if any one word could describe it, it would be *surrender*. You may ask, "How can I surrender my life?" It is surrendered in the same way that salvation comes to the sinner. There needs to be confession of sin and a complete yielding of every area of our lives, personalities, and wills to Jesus Christ—plus faith that Christ will accept that commitment.

It's not enough for us to be confirmed or to make a decision for Christ at an altar. We cannot walk successfully in the glow of that experience for the rest of our lives. We need to return and renew those vows and covenants with the Lord. We need to take inventory and have regular spiritual checkups.

Jesus said, "If anyone desires to come after Me, let him deny himself, and take up his cross daily, and follow Me" (Luke 9:23).
Daily surrender—that's the key to daily victory.

A Treasury of Faith

Yielded to God

Know ye not, that to whom ye yield yourselves servants to obey,
his servants ye are . . . ?

ROMANS 6:16, KJV

Of Eric Liddell, the missionary and great runner whose story is told in the film *Chariots of Fire*, someone has said, he was "ridiculously humble in victory, utterly generous in defeat." That's a good definition of what it means to be meek. Eric Liddell was fiercely competitive, determined to use his God-given abilities to the fullest. But his meekness, kindness, and gentle spirit won the admiration even of those he defeated.

Meekness involves being yielded. The word *yield* has two meanings. The first is negative, and the second is positive. On one hand it means "to relinquish, to abandon;" on the other hand, it also means "to give." This is in line with Jesus' words: "He who loses [or abandons] his life . . . will find it" (Matt. 10:39).

Those who submit to the will of God do not fight back at life. They learn the secret of yielding—of relinquishing and abandoning— their own lives and wills to Christ. And then He gives back to them a life that is far richer and fuller than anything they could ever have imagined.

A Treasury of Faith

The Resurrection and Life

He who believes in me will live, . . . and . . . will never die.

JOHN 11:25–26, NIV

We have three great enemies: sin, Satan, and death. Because Christ rose from the dead, we know that sin and death and Satan have been decisively defeated. And because Christ rose from the dead, we know there is life after death, and that if we belong to Him we need not fear death or hell.

Jesus said, "I am the resurrection and the life. He who believes in me will live, even though he dies; and whoever lives and believes in me will never die" (John 11:25–26, NIV). He also promised, "If I go and prepare a place for you, I will come back and take you to be with me that you also may be where I am" (John 14:3, NIV).

How hopeless our lives would be if these words were not true. Every cemetery and every grave site would be a mute witness to the futility and despair of human life. But His words are true! By God's power Jesus rose from the dead and hundreds became witnesses to His resurrection (see 1 Cor. 15:1–8). What a glorious hope we have because Jesus is alive!

A Treasury of Faith

The Privilege of Prayer

Ask, and you will receive, that your joy may be full.

JOHN 16:24

❦ What a privilege is ours: the privilege of prayer!
Just think of it: You and I have the incredible privilege of
approaching the God of the Universe, "the High and Lofty One who
inhabits eternity, whose name is Holy" (Isa. 57:15)! We can only do
this because Jesus Christ has opened the way.

We are to pray in times of adversity, lest we become faithless and
unbelieving. We are to pray in times of prosperity, lest we become
boastful and proud. We are to pray in times of danger, lest we become
fearful and doubting. We are to pray in times of security, lest we
become self-sufficient. Pray, believing, in the promise of God's Word
that "If we ask anything according to His will, He hears us"
(1 John 5:14).

Love Demonstrated

He loved us and sent His Son to be the propitiation for our sins.

1 JOHN 4:10

The word *love* is used to mean many different things. We say that we "love" the house that we have just bought or that we "love" a particular vacation spot or that we "love" a peanut butter and jelly sandwich. We also "love" a certain television program, and we "love" our husband or wife. Hopefully we don't love our spouse the same way we love a peanut butter and jelly sandwich!

The greatest love of all, however, is God's love for us—a love that showed itself in action. A friend once observed, "Love talked about is easily ignored, but love demonstrated is irresistible." The Bible says "God demonstrates His own love toward us, in that while we were still sinners, Christ died for us" (Rom. 5:8). Now that is *real* love! How will you respond to His love today?

A Treasury of Faith

Come Boldly

Ask, and it will be given you; seek, and you will find.

MATTHEW 7:7

Children are not bashful about asking for things. They would not be normal if they did not boldly make their needs known. God has said to His children, "Let us . . . come boldly to the throne of grace, that we may obtain mercy and find grace to help in time of need" (Heb. 4:16). God is keenly aware that we are dependent upon Him for life's necessities. It was for that reason that Jesus said, "Ask, and it will be given to you; seek, and you will find; knock, and it will be opened to you" (Matt. 7:7).

What is troubling you today? Is your heart burdened because of some problem that threatens to overcome you? Are you filled with anxiety and worry, wondering what will happen next? Listen—as a child of God through faith in Christ, you can turn these over to Christ, knowing that He loves you and is able to help you. Don't carry your burden any longer, but bring it "boldly to the throne of grace" —and leave it there.

A Treasury of Faith

A Certain Hope

Blessed is the man who trusts in the LORD, and whose hope is the LORD.
JEREMIAH 17:7

One of the great hymns of the church, "The Solid Rock," by Edward Mote and William Bradbury, begins, "My hope is built on nothing less, than Jesus' blood and righteousness; I dare not trust the sweetest frame, but wholly lean on Jesus' name. On Christ, the solid Rock, I stand; all other ground is sinking sand."

On what is your hope built? You may hope for a raise in pay at work. You may hope that you pass an exam at school. You may even hope that you win a contest you have entered. Such hopes are based on externals over which we have little control: a favorable view of our work by the boss, the "right" questions being asked by the professor, our name being drawn among thousands of entries.

But all these "hopes" fade into insignificance when compared with the greatest hope of all—our hope of salvation in Christ. And that hope is an absolute certainty, because it is based not on ourselves or our good works, but squarely on "Jesus' blood and righteousness."

A Treasury of Faith

Perfect Peace

Your faith has saved you. Go in peace.

LUKE 7:50

During the First World War, on Christmas Eve, the battlefield was strangely quiet. As the soft snow fell, the thoughts of the young men were of home and family.

Softly one lad began to hum "Silent Night." Others took up the chorus until the trenches resounded with the Christmas song. When they finished they were astonished to hear the song echoing from the trenches across no-man's-land: In their own tongue the other soldiers also sang "Silent Night." That night they were thinking of The Prince of Peace, the Christ of Christmas.

How different this world would be if we could unite together around that "Holy Infant so tender and mild." Earth can be as Heaven with Christ. Discord can be as peace when Christ is near. Midnight gloom can be transformed into noonday brightness when He abides with us. Full peace will come only when Christ returns. But until that day we can know His peace in our hearts and can be messengers of His peace in the world, as we commit our lives to Him.

A Treasury of Faith

Peace in the Storm

May the God of hope fill you with all joy and peace.

ROMANS 15:13

A wonderful old hymn says, "He gives us peace in the midst of a storm." In life we face all kinds of storms. We usually think of the personal "storms" that come our way—financial worries, problems in our marriage or family, illness, the betrayal of a friend, and so forth. But we face other kinds of storms that threaten to engulf us also: storms of materialism, storms of secularism, storms of moral degeneracy, storms of injustice, terrorism, and war.

Do you remember the violent storm that came upon Jesus and His disciples one night on the Sea of Galilee? His disciples grew panicky—but Jesus stayed fast asleep. He was at peace because He knew God was in control. He was at peace also because He was sovereign over the storm, and He knew it would vanish at His Word: "Peace, be still!" (Mark 4:39).

His Word still calms the turmoil in our lives. Is some storm making you fearful today? Stay close to Jesus, for His Word brings peace.

A Treasury of Faith

God Never Changes

God is Spirit, and those who worship Him
must worship in spirit and truth.

JOHN 4:24

I was reared in a small Presbyterian church in Charlotte, North Carolina. Before I was ten years of age my mother made me memorize the "Shorter Catechism," a summary of basic Christian beliefs in the form of questions and answers. In the catechism we were asked to define God. The answer we learned was, "God is a Spirit—infinite, eternal, and unchangeable."

Those three words beautifully describe God. He is infinite—not body-bound. Eternal—He has no beginning and no ending. He is unchangeable—never changing, never capricious, never unreliable. As the Bible says, with God "there is no variation or shadow of turning" (James 1:17). He is forever self-existent.

People change, fashions change, conditions and circumstances change, but God never changes. His love never changes. His holiness never changes. His purpose never changes. His glory never changes. He is the same yesterday, today, and forever.

Can you think of any reason *not* to trust Him? Neither can I!

A Treasury of Faith

Lord and Master

You call me Teacher and Lord, and you say well, for so I am.

JOHN 13:13

I wonder if you've ever thought about the incredible number of messages that rain down on us every day: television ads, e-mails, phone calls, magazines, junk mail, videos, billboards, conversations— the list is almost endless.

How many of those shape our thinking? How many of them subtly convince us that the road to happiness is really paved with possessions, or beauty, or money, or fame, or any of a hundred other things? How many of them persuade us that the most important thing in life is financial success, or the esteem of others, or power, or sex? It's hard to resist the cumulative impact of so many messages.

But God says our thinking must be shaped by His truth. What this world calls valuable, God calls worthless. What this world scorns, God exalts. "My thoughts are not your thoughts, nor are your ways My ways," (Isa. 55:8). Jesus said, "You call me Teacher and Lord, and you say well, for so I am." Is He *your* Teacher and Lord—or is the world?

A Treasury of Faith

79

The Anthem of His Name

God also has . . . given Him the name which is above every name.

PHILIPPIANS 2:9

Over two thousand years ago, on a night the world has come to call Christmas, a young Jewish maiden went through the experience countless mothers had before her: She brought forth a child. But this birth was like no other in the history of the human race. For one thing, this Child had no human father. As the angel had promised, "The Holy Spirit will come upon you, and the power of the Highest will overshadow you" (Luke 1:35). In humble obedience the Virgin Mary responded, "Let it be to me according to your word" (Luke 1:38).

But it also was like no other birth because of the One who was born. This was no ordinary child. This was the unique Son of God, sent from Heaven to save us from our sins. Amid the glitter and busyness of the season, don't lose sight of the miracle of that first Christmas. With the wise men, let us fall down and worship Him (Matt. 2:11).

Serving God Forever

Because of His great love . . .
He . . . made us alive together with Christ.

EPHESIANS 2:4–5

Your life may seem monotonous and filled with drudgery. Yet remember, if you are a Christian, you are not working for an hour or for a day but for eternity. When this body of corruption shall take on immortality, another part of our work will begin, for the Scripture teaches that God's servants shall serve Him forever. The difference is that in Heaven we will never grow bored or weary!

Some time ago a man said to me, "You might be mistaken, for no one has ever come back from the grave to tell us." I replied, "Sir, that's exactly where you are wrong. Someone has returned—His name is Jesus Christ, our Lord."

That makes all the difference! Because Christ is alive, we have "an inheritance incorruptible and undefiled . . . reserved in heaven" (1 Pet. 1:4). And this helps us persevere, even when life seems dull.

A Treasury of Faith

Our Great Assurance

Let us draw near with a true heart in full assurance of faith.

HEBREWS 10:22

Disregard your feelings when you come to Christ. You aren't saved by your feelings; you are saved by Christ. Feelings come and go, but Christ remains.

Only the facts matter—the fact that Jesus Christ died for your sins and rose again; the fact that if you have committed your life to Him, He has promised to forgive you and save you. The Bible says, "God has given us eternal life, and this life is in His Son. He who has the Son has life" (1 John 5:11–12).

That is God's promise to you—and He cannot lie. Your feelings will lie to you—and Satan may even use them to convince you God has abandoned you or that you have lost your salvation. But remember: "There is no truth in him. When he lies, he speaks his native language, for he is a liar and the father of lies" (John 8:44, NIV). How wonderful to know our faith is based on God's truth, and not our feelings!

A Treasury of Faith

God's Abiding Presence

*The love of God has been poured out in our hearts by
the Holy Spirit who was given to us.*

ROMANS 5:5

Years ago when I traveled to Europe to preach I liked to travel by
sea, to enjoy the five days of relative quiet on the ship.

On one of my voyages Captain Anderson of the *United States* took
me down to see the ship's gyroscope. He said, "When the sea is rough,
the gyroscope helps to keep the ship on an even keel. Though the waves
may reach tremendous proportions, the gyroscope helps to stabilize the
vessel and maintain a high degree of equilibrium."

As I listened, I thought how like the gyroscope is the Holy Spirit
in our hearts. Let the storms of life break over our heads. Let the enemy
Satan come in like a flood. Let the waves of sorrow, suffering, temptation, and testing be unleashed upon us. Our souls will be kept on
an even keel and in perfect peace when the Holy Spirit dwells in our
hearts. He comforts us with God's abiding presence, and assures us that
God's promises are true.

A Treasury of Faith

The King of Kings

A scepter of righteousness is the scepter of Your kingdom.

PSALM 45:6

From his very birth Christ was recognized as King. Something about him inspired allegiance, loyalty and homage. Wise men brought Him gifts. Shepherds fell down and worshiped Him. Herod, realizing that there is never room for two thrones in one kingdom, sought His life. As Jesus began His ministry, His claims upon people's lives were total and absolute. He allowed no divided loyalty. He demanded and received complete adoration and devotion. Mature men and women left their businesses and gave themselves in complete obedience to Him. Many of them gave their lives, pouring out the last full measure of devotion.

His words caused even His most avowed enemies to say, "No man ever spoke like this Man!" (John 7:46). And yet He was more than a poet, more than a statesman, more than a physician. We cannot understand Christ until we understand that He was the King of kings and the Lord of lords. Like Thomas, our only response must be to bow down and confess, "My Lord and my God!" (John 20:28).

A Treasury of Faith

Christ's Promise

I will be with you always,
to the very end of the age.

MATTHEW 28:20, NIV

These words are Christ's promise to all His disciples, and it is a promise that is marvelously inclusive. No situation is excluded; no challenge is omitted. Dr. Handley Moule, the noted Greek scholar and Anglican Bishop of Durham (England) in another generation, maintained that the word *always* could be paraphrased to mean, "I am with you all the days, all day long." That means we can count on Christ's presence not only every day, but every moment of every day.
Of the *fact* of His presence there can be no doubt,
for His Word cannot fail.

What we need is to cultivate the *sense* of His presence,
every day, every hour, every moment. This happens as we speak to Him
in worship and prayer, and listen to Him speak to us through
His Word, the Bible.

A Treasury of Faith

Serving Eternally

You have a better and an enduring possession for yourselves in heaven.

HEBREWS 10:34

Some people think Heaven will be dull and boring, but nothing could be further from the truth. The Father's house will be a happy home because there will be work to do there. John wrote in Revelation 22:3, "His servants shall serve Him." Each one will be given exactly the task that suits his powers, his tastes, and his abilities. And the Father's house will be a happy home because friends will be there. Have you ever been to a strange place and had the joy of seeing a familiar face? Not one of us who enters the Father's house will feel lonely or strange, for we who have put our trust in Christ are part of His family, sharing Heaven's joys forever with all our brothers and sisters in Christ.

Alexander MacLaren described Heaven this way: "The joys of heaven are not the joys of passive contemplation, of dreamy remembrance, . . . but they are described thus, 'They rest not night or day,' and 'His servants serve Him and see His face.'" In the midst of earth's turmoil, keep your eyes on Heaven!

A Treasury of Faith

Accept God's Freedom

Draw near to God and He will draw near to you.

JAMES 4:8

One day a little child was playing with a valuable vase. He put his hand into it and could not take it out. His father, too, tried his best to get the little boy's hand out, but all in vain. They were thinking of breaking the vase when the father said, "Now, my son, make one more try. Open your hand and hold your fingers out straight as you see me doing and then pull."

To the father's astonishment the little fellow said, "Oh no, Daddy. I couldn't put my fingers out like that because if I did I would drop my penny." Smile if you will—but thousands of us are like that little boy, so busy holding on to the world's worthless trifles that we cannot accept God's freedom. What "trifle" is keeping you from God? A sin you won't let go of? An unworthy goal you are determined to reach? A dishonorable relationship you won't give up? I beg you to drop that trifle in your heart. Surrender! Let go and let God have His way in your life.

A Treasury of Faith

The Greatest Security

He who dwells in the secret place of the Most High shall abide under the shadow of the Almighty.

PSALM 91:1

Someone has said that the only certainty in life is uncertainty—and it is true. Governments collapse, stock markets plummet, wars destroy, disasters strike, relationships end. As the writer of Hebrews put it, "Here we have no continuing city" (Heb. 13:14). Yet deep in the human heart is a yearning for security—a yearning that will not go away. We know we need a solid foundation to life, a foundation that cannot be shaken. Where will it be found?

Only God never changes. His love does not change, and neither do His promises. That is why we can look to Him for the security and stability we all seek. King David knew the secret: "He who dwells in the secret place of the Most High shall abide under the shadow of the Almighty."

Salvation is not an occasional, vague feeling of God's presence. It is actually dwelling with God, secure in His presence forever. Is *your* security in Christ?

A Treasury of Faith

Walk with God

My eyes shall be on the faithful of the land,
that they may dwell with me.

PSALM 101:6

Walk with God as Noah did; when the flood came, Noah was saved amidst the scorn and rejection of his neighbors. Walk with God as Moses did in the solitude of the desert; when the hour of judgment fell upon Egypt, Moses was prepared to lead his people to victory. Walk with God as David did as a shepherd boy; when he was called to rule his people he was prepared for the task of kingship. Walk with God as Daniel and his three young friends did in the palace of Babylon's king; when the fiery furnace and the lion's den came, God was beside them and delivered them.

No, God didn't always deliver His saints from adversity or even death, nor does He today. But because they had learned to trust Him in the light, they were prepared to follow Him in the darkness. God has not promised to deliver us *from* trouble, but He has promised to go with us *through* the trouble.

"Yea, though I walk through the valley of the shadow of death, I will fear no evil; for You are with me" (Ps. 23:4).

A Treasury of Faith

Crown Him the Lord of life,
who triumphed over the grave,
And rose victorious in the strife
for those He came to save.

Victory in Jesus

Thanks be to God, who gives us the victory
through our Lord Jesus Christ.
1 CORINTHIANS 15:57, NRSV

Haydn, the great musician, was once asked why his church music was so cheerful. He replied, "When I think upon God, my heart is so full of joy that the notes dance and leap, as it were, from my pen, and since God has given me a cheerful heart, it will be pardoned me that I serve Him with a cheerful spirit."

Haydn had discovered the secret to lasting joy: "I think on God." Looking at our circumstances won't bring us lasting joy. It may even make us depressed or angry. But when we "think on God"—when we turn our minds and hearts to His power and His love for us, we can't help but be joyful. Paul said, "Set your mind on things above, not on things on the earth" (Col. 3:2). Discouragement flees in the face of joy.

Every day brings battles and temptations. But the strength we need for conquering them comes from Christ. We can do like the little girl who said that when the devil came knocking with a temptation, she just sent Jesus to the door!

A Treasury of Faith

Living a Peaceable Life

Lead a quiet and peaceable life in all godliness and reverence.

1 TIMOTHY 2:2

As Christians we aren't to isolate ourselves from the world in which we live. We are part of society, and we share in its difficulties, problems, and hopes. The Bible has much to say about our social responsibility. The Old Testament prophets condemned those who ignored the poor and exploited the weak. Not that it is easy. As Christians, we know human society is affected by sin, and any effort to improve society will always be incomplete and imperfect. We will never build a Utopia on earth.

But we must do all we can to alleviate suffering, and to strike at the root causes of injustice, racial prejudice, hunger, and violence. We are to work for a peaceable life and human dignity for others. Why? Because God loves this suffering world. Jesus saw the crowds and "was moved with compassion" (Matt. 9:36).

Christ is concerned about the whole person—including the society in which that person lives. Do we share His concern?

A Treasury of Faith

Joy on the Journey

The joy of the LORD is your strength.

NEHEMIAH 8:10

Some people have a warped idea of living the Christian life. Seeing talented, successful Christians, they attempt to imitate them. For them, the grass on the other side of the fence is always greener. But when they discover that their own gifts are different or their contributions are more modest (or even invisible), they collapse in discouragement and overlook genuine opportunities that are open to them. They have forgotten that they are here to serve Christ, not themselves.

Be like the apostle Paul and say, "None of these things move me." Few men suffered as Paul did, yet he learned how to live above his circumstances—even in a prison cell. You can do the same. The key is to realize you are here to serve Christ, not yourself.

God does not promise us an easy life, free of troubles, trials, difficulties, and temptations. He never promises that life will be perfect. He does not call His children to a playground, but to a battleground. In the midst of it all, when we serve Christ, we truly discover that "the joy of the LORD is [our] strength."

A Treasury of Faith

Resting Faith

The testing of your faith produces patience.

Dwight L. Moody was fond of pointing out that there are three kinds of faith in Jesus Christ: *struggling faith*, which is like a man floundering and fearful in deep water; *clinging faith*, which is like a man hanging to the side of a boat; and *resting faith*, which finds a man safe inside the boat—strong and secure enough to reach out his hand to help someone else.

Notice each man had faith. Each knew the boat was his only hope. But only one had a *resting* faith. Only one had discovered he could actually be *in* the boat —where all he had to do was rest. This is the kind of faith God wants us to have—a faith that trusts Him totally. But sometimes we discover its reality only after we have endured a struggling or clinging faith. Sometimes we only realize we can get *in* the boat when the storm rages and we cry out to God with new faith.

Then our Savior graciously extends His hand and says, "Come to Me . . . and I will give you rest" (Matt. 11:28).

A Treasury of Faith

95

Glorious Responsibilities

If anyone serves Me, him My father will honor.

JOHN 12:26

Young people seek adventure and excitement; but youth wants more—it wants something to believe in; it wants a cause to give itself to and a flag to follow. Without a purpose greater than themselves, young people know they will end up with empty hearts and meaningless lives. The only cause that is big enough to satisfy the yearning of our hearts is the cause of Jesus Christ; and its flag is the blood-stained body that was lifted on the Cross of Calvary for the redemption of the world.

This invitation to discipleship is the most thrilling cause we could ever imagine. Think of it: The God of the universe invites us to become His partners in reclaiming the world for Him! We can each have a part, using the unique gifts and opportunities God has given us.

Christ's call is for us to be His disciples every day.
How are you responding to His call?

A Treasury of Faith

White as Snow

Wash me, and I shall be whiter than snow.

PSALM 51:7

Snow is so white that one can see almost anything that is dropped
on it, even at great distances. We can take the whitest object we can
find, like newly washed clothing, but when we place it next to snow
it still looks dirty by comparison. Our lives are like that. At times, we
may think of ourselves as morally good and decent; we are content that
"we are not like other men." But compared to God's purity,
we are defiled and filthy.

In spite of our sins and uncleanness, God still loves us. And
because He loves us, He decided to provide for us a purity we could
never attain on our own. That is why He gave His Son, Jesus Christ,
to die for us on the Cross. Only when our sins have been washed in
the blood of Jesus Christ will we appear as white as snow in the eyes of
God. Thank God today that you are now "whiter than snow," because
"you were washed . . . in the name of the Lord Jesus and by the
Spirit of our God" (1 Cor. 6:11).

A Treasury of Faith

The Divine Flame

You shall receive power when the Holy Spirit
has come upon you; and you shall be my witnesses.

ACTS 1:8

Simon Peter was so spiritually weak before Pentecost that, in
spite of his bragging to the contrary, he swore and denied Christ. He
was cowed by the crowd, shamed by a little maid, and took his place
with the enemies of Christ. But see him after he has been baptized
with fire—the fire of the Holy Spirit! He stands boldly before the same
rabble that had crucified Jesus, looks into their faces, and fearlessly pro-
claims the good news of salvation (see Acts 2:36). Peter, the weak, was
transformed into Peter, the rock.

So it was with the early disciples. The Holy Spirit changed them
from ordinary individuals into firebrands for God. Their faith
and zeal started a conflagration that spread throughout the Roman
Empire. Their secret? Total submission to Jesus Christ and
His will. What keeps you from being used of God to touch your
world for Christ?

A Treasury of Faith

Reach for His Hand

The LORD, He is the One who goes before you. He will be with you.

DEUTERONOMY 31:8

Once many years ago when I was going through a dark period I prayed and prayed, but the heavens seemed to be brass. I felt as though God had disappeared and that I was alone with my trial and burden. It was a dark night for my soul.

I wrote my mother about the experience and will never forget her reply: "Son, there are many times when God withdraws to test your faith. He wants you to trust Him in the darkness. Now, Son, reach up by faith in the fog and you will find that His hand will be there." In tears I knelt by my bed and experienced an overwhelming sense of God's presence.

Whether or not we feel God's presence when our way seems dark, by faith we know He is there. You can stake your life on His promise: "I will never leave you nor forsake you" (Heb. 13:5).

A Treasury of Faith

The Hope of the Centuries

*It is good that one should hope and wait quietly
for the salvation of the LORD.*

LAMENTATIONS 3:26

The promised coming of Christ has been the great hope of believers down through the centuries. The ancient Nicene Creed affirms, "He shall come again with glory." Charles Wesley wrote 7,000 hymns; 5,000 mention the coming of Christ. As the Archbishop of Canterbury crowned Queen Elizabeth II, he stated, "I give thee, O Sovereign Lady, this crown to wear until He who reserves the right to wear it shall return."

But until that time, our world remains in the grip of violence and despair. One noted columnist summed it up this way: "For us all, the world is disorderly and dangerous; ungoverned, and apparently ungovernable." Some day, however, the King will return. Some day the heavens will shout, "The kingdoms of this world have become the kingdoms of our Lord and of His Christ, and He shall reign forever and ever!" (Rev. 11:15). Christ alone is the answer to the burdens of our hearts and the hopelessness of our world.

A Treasury of Faith

Power to Change the World

You are my hope, O LORD God;
You are my trust from my youth.

PSALM 71:5

We still wrestle with the same problems that preoccupied Plato and Aristotle centuries ago: Where did we come from? Why are we here? Where are we going? We search for answers, but the signs all seem to say "no exit."

But the Cross boldly stands against the confusion of our world, a beacon of hope in the midst of darkness and doubt. In the Cross, Christ not only bridged the gap between God and us, but there we find the answers to life's deepest questions. There we discover our true identity: forgiven sinners who now belong to God. There we discover our true destiny: a glorious eternity with God in Heaven. There we discover our true purpose: to love God and serve Him with all our might.

Never underestimate what Christ did for us through the Cross. By it our salvation was won, and by it our lives—and our world—can be transformed. What difference does the Cross make in your life?

A Treasury of Faith

A Gentle Kindness

*The Lord's servant must not be
quarrelsome but kindly to every one.*

2 TIMOTHY 2:24, NRSV

Jesus was a gentle and compassionate person. When He came
into the world, there were few hospitals, few places of refuge for the
poor, few homes for orphans. There were no hospitals to treat the
mentally ill, no shelters for the homeless. In comparison to today, it was
a cruel world.

Christ changed all that. He healed the sick, fed the hungry, and
opened the eyes of the blind. He commanded His disciples, "Love your
neighbor as yourself" (Matt. 19:19), and taught them to observe what
we have come to call the Golden Rule: "In everything, do to others
what you would have them do to you" (Matt. 7:12, NIV). Wherever true
Christianity has gone, His followers have performed acts of kindness,
love, and gentleness.

Do others see Christ's gentleness and compassion in you?

Discover God's Grace

We conducted ourselves in the world . . .by the grace of God.
2 CORINTHIANS 1:12

Is God's grace really sufficient in times of trouble? Can it sustain us in the midst of life's storms?

Yes—but to be honest, sometimes it's hard for us to rely on God's grace instead of ourselves. We think we have to grab control of our lives, and believe the responsibility for shaping our future must be in our hands.

When troubles come, therefore, we resist them instead of depending on God to see us through. Alexander Maclaren, the distinguished British preacher of another generation, once wrote, "What disturbs us in this world is not trouble, but our opposition to trouble."

Put God to the test when troubles come. He won't let you down. In the midst of a painful illness Paul begged God to intervene and take it away. But God replied "My grace is sufficient for you" (2 Cor. 12:9). It was for Paul, and it will be for you.

A Treasury of Faith

The Living Christ

It is no longer I who live, but Christ lives in me.

GALATIANS 2:20

Jesus Christ was crucified between two thieves on a rugged cross on Calvary, just outside Jerusalem. Think of it: The very Son of God came down from Heaven and "humbled Himself and became obedient to the point of death, even the death of the cross" (Phil. 2:8).

Jesus gave His head to the crown of thorns for us. He gave His face to the human spittle for us. He gave His cheeks and His beard to be plucked out for us. He gave His back to the lash for us. He gave His side to the spear for us. He gave His hands and feet to the spikes for us. He gave His blood for us. Jesus Christ, dying in our place, taking our sins on that cross, is God's love in action.

But that's not the end of the story. He rose again, and He is the living Christ. If Christ is not alive, there is no hope for any of us. But He is alive! And because He is, "he is able to save completely those who come to God through him, because he always lives to intercede for them" (Heb. 7:25, NIV). Hallelujah!

A Treasury of Faith

The Work of Angels

*Bless the LORD, you His angels, who excel in strength,
who do His word.*

PSALM 103:20

It's natural to concentrate on what the angels do for us, these who
are "sent to serve those who will inherit salvation" (Heb. 1:14, NIV).
But the Bible indicates the angels do much more than that.
Especially, we are told, the angels unite in constant praise to God,
giving glory to His name and rejoicing in His holiness and perfection.
"Bless the LORD, you His angels."

Isaiah is granted a vision of heaven, where the angelic hosts proclaim,
"Holy, holy, holy is the LORD of hosts; the whole earth is full of His
glory!" (Isa. 6:3). John sees "many angels around the throne . . . saying
with a loud voice: 'Worthy is the Lamb who was slain'" (Rev. 5:11–12).
Jesus said there is "rejoicing in the presence of the angels of God over one
sinner who repents" (Luke 15:10 NIV).

Are they not examples to us? Shouldn't rejoicing and praise be
hallmarks of our lives? Praise will banish darkness, and bring us closer
to God. Martin Luther once said, "Come, let us sing a psalm and
drive away the devil!"

A Treasury of Faith

The Summit of Love

How great is the love the Father has lavished on us,
that we should be called children of God!

1 JOHN 3:1, NIV

Mary and Joseph deeply loved the Child God gave them,
even becoming refugees to spare His life when King Herod
tried to kill Him (Matt. 2:13).

But their love was almost nothing compared with the infinite love
of God for His Son. The Bible declares, "The Father loves the Son, and
has given all things into His hand" (John 3:35). Can you even begin to
imagine the Father's emotions that first Christmas as His dearly loved
Son left Heaven for earth, knowing He would one day go to the Cross,
"despised and rejected by men, a Man of sorrows and acquainted
with grief" (Isa. 53:3)?

We rightly focus on God's love for us. But don't lose sight of what it
cost the Father to send His beloved Son into the world. Why did He do
it? Because "God so loved the world that He gave His only begotten Son,
that whoever believes in Him should not perish but have everlasting life"
(John 3:16). God loves the Son—and He loves you as well.

Godly Thoughts

Be transformed by the renewing of your mind.

ROMANS 12:2

The Bible teaches that our minds are to be brought under the control of Christ. The reason? How we act will be determined by how we think. If God is to change our lives, He must first change our minds. The human mind cannot be a vacuum. It will be filled either with good or evil. It will be filled either with Christ or with carnality. What will make the difference?

It depends on us, and on what we allow to enter our minds. Negatively, our minds must be turned away from evil. We must be careful what kind of television programs we see, what kind of books we read, the things that occupy our thoughts. But it isn't enough to put bad thoughts out of our minds. Positively, they must be replaced with good thoughts—thoughts that are shaped by God and His word, by prayer and worship, by fellowship with other Christians.

Deliberately turn away from every evil thought today and ask God to fill your mind instead with Himself from this moment on.

A Treasury of Faith

Coronation Day

Blessed is the man who endures trial for . . .
he will receive the crown of life.

JAMES 1:12, RSV

To the Christian, death is said in the Bible to be a coronation.
The picture here is that of a regal prince who, after his struggles and
conquests in an alien land, returns to his native country and court to be
crowned and honored for his deeds.

The Bible says we are pilgrims and strangers in a foreign land. This
world is not our home; our citizenship is in heaven. And some day all
our battles on this earth will be over, and we will enter that Heavenly
Home. To the one who has been faithful Christ will give a crown of life.
Paul said, "There is laid up for me the crown of righteousness, which
the Lord, the righteous Judge, will give to me on that day, and not to
me only but also to all who have loved His appearing" (2 Tim. 4:8).

When D. L. Moody was dying, he looked up to heaven and said,
"Earth is receding, heaven is opening, this is my coronation day." Never
forget: If you are a Christian, you are a child of the King!

Enjoying God's Presence

In Your presence is fullness of joy.

PSALM 16:11

Have you ever watched a young couple communicate their love for each other without even saying a word? Maybe you have experienced it yourself. Every glance, every touch, every smile conveys love. People deeply in love find absolute bliss simply being in each other's presence.

In the same way, simply being in the presence of God brings us great joy. It happens as we listen to Him speak in His Word; it happens as we pray. But it also happens as we simply enjoy His presence—meditating on His goodness, delighting in the beauty of His creation, rejoicing in the life of a new baby or the surprise of an unexpected blessing. The Bible says, "Be still, and know that I am God" (Ps. 46:10).

Some day we will be in His presence forever; the Bible says, "God Himself will be with them" (Rev. 21:3). What joy that will be! But in the meantime, delight in His presence right now, for He is with you every hour of the day.

A Treasury of Faith

Sufficient Grace

My grace is sufficient for you.

2 CORINTHIANS 12:9

The prayer of Jesus in the Garden of Gethsemane is perhaps the greatest, most moving prayer ever uttered. In it our Lord asked that the cup of crucifixion, which was about to be thrust upon Him, might be taken away. But then, in the very next breath He said, "Nevertheless, not as I will, but as You will" (Matt. 26:39). What a prayer! What strength! What power!

When the apostle Paul asked God to remove his "thorn in the flesh," God did not remove it, saying instead, "My grace is sufficient for you" (2 Cor. 12:9). Rather than complain or become angry at God, Paul joyfully submitted to God's will. He discovered that God's grace truly was sufficient, even in the midst of pain.

Christ desires to be with you in whatever crisis you may find yourself. Call upon His name. See if He will not do as He promised He would. He may not make your problems go away, but He will give you the power to deal with them and to overcome them by His grace.

A Treasury of Faith